Favorite Authors

Mo Willems

by Abby Colich

CAPSTONE PRESS
a capstone imprint

First Facts are published by Capstone Press,
1710 Roe Crest Drive, North Mankato, Minnesota 56003
www.capstonepub.com

Library of Congress Cataloging-in-Publication Data
Colich, Abby.
  Mo Willems / by Abby Colich.
     pages cm.—(First Facts. Your Favorite Authors)
  Includes bibliographical references and index.
  Summary: "Presents the life and career of Mo Willems, including his childhood, education, and milestones as a best-selling children's author"—Provided by publisher.
  ISBN 978-1-4765-3157-1 (library binding)
  ISBN 978-1-4765-3444-2 (paperback)
  ISBN 978-1-4765-3434-3 (eBook PDF)
  1. Willems, Mo—Juvenile literature. 2. Illustrators—United States—Biography—Juvenile literature. I. Title.
  NC975.5.W519C65 2014
  741.6'42—dc23
  [B]   2013003120

Editorial Credits
Christopher L. Harbo, editor; Tracy Davies McCabe and Gene Bentdahl, designers; Marcie Spence, media researcher; Kathy McColley, production specialist

Photo Credits
Alamy Images: Everett Collection Historical 7 (left); AP Images: Diane Bondareff/AP Images for Disney Publishing Worldwide, 15; Capstone Press: Michael Byers, cover, 17 (bottom); Capstone Studio: Karon Dubke, 13 (top), 19; Courtesy of Mo Willems, 5 (top), 7 (right), 9, 17 (top), 21; Getty Images: Scott Gries/ImageDirect, 11; Newscom: infusny-236/Walter McBride, 10; Shutterstock: s_oleg, 5 (bottom), 13 (bottom)

Printed in the United States of America in North Mankato, Minnesota.
092015   009189R

Table of Contents

Chapter 1: Pigeon Is Born

Mo Willems had a successful career writing for TV. But he really wanted to create a children's book. He traveled to Oxford, England, to get ideas in 1997.

Willems didn't like any of the stories he wrote while he stayed in Oxford. Instead, he doodled a pigeon in his sketchbook. At the time Willems didn't realize that this pigeon would soon be famous.

Willems in Oxford, England

5

Chapter 2: Doodling and TV Writing

Mo Willems was born February 11, 1968, in Des Plaines, Illinois. His family moved to New Orleans, Louisiana, in 1972. His parents were Dutch **immigrants**. Mo was an only child. Growing up he loved reading comics and doodling. The first character Mo created was named Lazer Brain. He was a space hero who lost his brain in a space accident.

---

immigrant—a person who leaves one country and settles in another

Love of *Peanuts*

As a child Mo Willems really loved the *Peanuts* comic strip. He even wrote a letter to *Peanuts* creator Charles Schulz. Mo said he wanted Schulz's job when Schulz died!

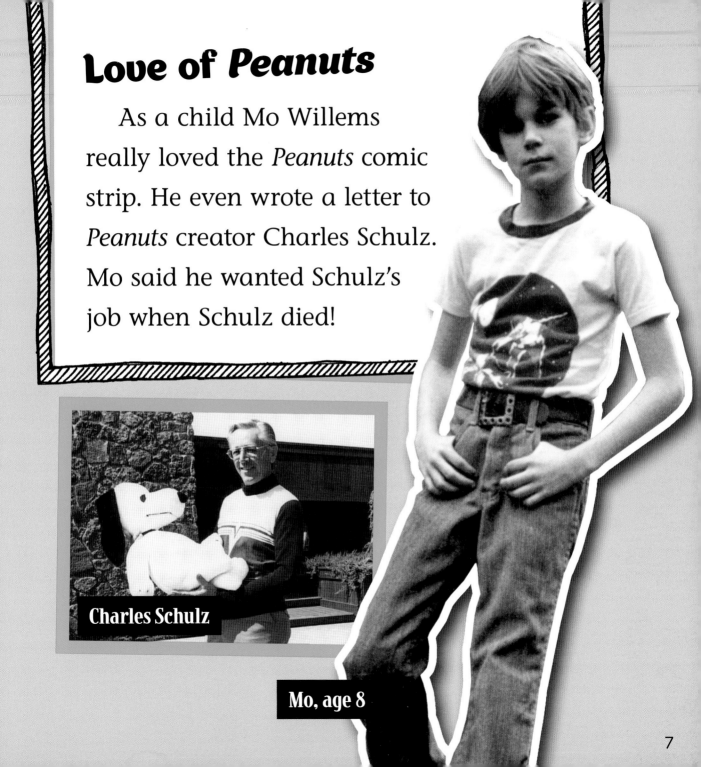

Charles Schulz

Mo, age 8

After high school Willems moved to London, England. For a short time he did **stand-up comedy**. Then he moved to New York. He studied film and **animation** at New York University's Tisch School of the Arts. After he finished college in 1990, Willems traveled around the world for one year. He drew a sketch every day. These drawings were **published** in 2006. The book was called *You Can Never Find a Rickshaw When It Monsoons.*

Willems' studio in 1994

stand-up comedy—a type of entertainment in which a person tells jokes in front of a live audience

animation—cartoons made by quickly presenting drawings, one after another, so that the characters seem to be moving

publish—to produce and distribute a book, magazine, or newspaper so that people can buy it

Willems became a writer for *Sesame Street* in 1993. He won six **Emmy** awards before leaving in 2002. Willems worked for other TV series too. He created *Sheep in the Big City* on Cartoon Network. He was also head writer for *Codename: Kids Next Door* on Cartoon Network.

Emmy—an award given for work on a television show

"It was at *Sesame Street* that I learned how to write for children. ... By the time I was gone I realized this was where I wanted my career to be."—Mo Willems

Chapter 3:
Many Characters and Many Books

Willems' career as a children's author started when an **agent** saw his pigeon sketchbook. She thought it would make a good book. *Don't Let the Pigeon Drive the Bus!* was published in 2003. The book was a best-seller. It received several awards, including a Caldecott Honor. This award is given to the best picture books of the year.

---

agent—someone who helps an author find a publisher

13

The Pigeon book was just the beginning of Willems' success. *Knuffle Bunny: A Cautionary Tale* was published in 2004. This first book in the Knuffle Bunny series stars Trixie, named after Willems' daughter. In the story Trixie becomes upset when she loses her stuffed bunny. *Knuffle Bunny* was a huge hit. It was made into a musical. Willems even wrote the words for the **script** and songs.

---

script—the story for a play, movie, or television show

More Than Just Books

Willems has worked on several projects based on his characters. The program *Don't Let the Pigeon Run This App!* lets readers create their own Pigeon stories on an iPad.

Willems released the first of several Elephant and Piggie books in 2007. In the books Willems uses **themes** that are important to both kids and grown-ups. These themes include friendship, love, and jealousy. For example, *Listen to My Trumpet!* focuses on honesty and kindness. Elephant must kindly tell Piggie that she is not a very good trumpet player.

---

theme—main idea that the story addresses

"I don't want to preach. ... I just want to show and let the kids figure out what the books mean for them."—Mo Willems

Willems' books continue to be best-sellers. His Pigeon book *Duckling Gets a Cookie!?* came out in 2012. It rose to the top of *The New York Times* best-seller list. That same year, *Goldilocks and the Three Dinosaurs* hit bookstores. In it Willems put a funny spin on a classic children's story. In 2013 he released *That Is Not a Good Idea!* This picture book stars a plump goose and a hungry fox.

19

Chapter 4: Draw and Be Silly!

Mo Willems' characters are loved all over the world. Pigeon, Knuffle Bunny, Elephant, Piggie, and many others have starred in dozens of his books. But Willems wants his readers to do more than just read. He wants children and adults to have fun and act silly. He also wants readers to draw their own stories using his simple characters.

"Reading is only part of the experience. I want those characters to become so alive that kids create their own comics and their own books, using my characters."—Mo Willems

Willems wearing a paper robot mask

Timeline

1968   born February 11 in Des Plaines, Illinois

1990   graduates from Tisch School of the Arts in New York

1993   starts working as a writer for *Sesame Street*

1997   gets married to Cheryl Camp in Brooklyn, New York; travels to Oxford, England, to get ideas for children's books

2001   daughter, Trixie, is born

2002   leaves his job with *Sesame Street*

2003   *Don't Let the Pigeon Drive the Bus!* is published

2004   *Knuffle Bunny: A Cautionary Tale* is published

2006   *You Can Never Find a Rickshaw When It Monsoons* is published

2007   the first of the Elephant and Piggie books is published

2010   *Knuffle Bunny: A Cautionary Musical* opens in New York; the Cat the Cat series is published

2011   *Don't Let the Pigeon Run This App!* is released for the iPad

2012   *Goldilocks and the Three Dinosaurs* is published

2013   *That Is Not a Good Idea!* is published

Glossary

agent (AY-juhnt)—someone who helps an author find a publisher

animation (a-nuh-MAY-shuhn)—cartoons made by quickly presenting drawings, one after another, so that the characters seem to be moving

Emmy (EM-ee)—an award given for work on a television show

graduate (GRAJ-oo-ate)—to finish a course of study in school and receive a diploma

immigrant (IM-uh-gruhnt)—a person who leaves one country and settles in another

publish (PUHB-lish)—to produce and distribute a book, magazine, or newspaper so that people can buy it

script (SKRIPT)—the story for a play, movie, or television show

stand-up comedy (STAND-UHP KOM-uh-dee)—a type of entertainment in which a person tells jokes in front of a live audience

theme (THEEM)—main idea that the story addresses

Read More

Fandel, Jennifer. *You Can Write Awesome Stories*. You Can Write. North Mankato, Minn.: Capstone Press, 2012.

Llanas, Sheila Griffin. *Picture Yourself Writing Fiction: Using Photos to Inspire Writing*. See It, Write It. Mankato, Minn.: Capstone Press, 2012.

Internet Sites

FactHound offers a safe, fun way to find Internet sites related to this book. All of the sites on FactHound have been researched by our staff.

Here's all you do:

Visit *www.facthound.com*

Type in this code: 9781476531571

Index

Super-cool stuff! Check out projects, games and lots more at **www.capstonekids.com**